“No!”

For Roger

Also by Tony Kenyon
Oops! says Olly Bear
Hello! says Olly Bear

By Ruth Louise Symes and Tony Kenyon
Floppy Ears

First published in Great Britain in 2003
by Orion Children's Books
This paperback edition published in 2004
by Dolphin Paperbacks
a division of the Orion Publishing Group Ltd
Orion House
5 Upper St Martin's Lane
London WC2H 9EA

A catalogue record for this book is available from the British Library

Printed and bound in Italy

ISBN 1 84255 163 9

No! says Olly Bear

TONY KENYON

Dolphin

It was breakfast time.
“Eat up your porridge, Olly,” said Mum.

"No!" said Olly.
"I don't like porridge."

Olly got down from the table.

Mum lifted
Baby Bear out of
her high chair.

"There!" she said. "Now you can play together."

"No!" said Olly Bear. "She's too little."

“Who’s coming to the shops?”
said Olly’s dad.
“I am!” said Olly.

“I’ll come too, with the baby,”
said Olly’s mum.

"NO! I don't want her to come," said Olly.

Mum and Dad did the shopping, while Olly stumped along behind.

"I want to go home," said Olly.

"When we're ready," said Dad.

“I’m hungry,” said Olly.

“Would you like a bun?” said Mum.

"I don't want a bun, I want a doughnut," said Olly. "And I want to go to the park."

"Not today," said Dad. "We're going straight home."

Olly sulked. He wouldn't hold Dad's paw.

He wouldn't push the buggy.

And when they got home, he wouldn't help Mum unpack the shopping.

Then Olly saw the back door was open . . .

. . . and he slipped outside.

Olly ran round and round the garden.
There was no one to tell him what to do.

And there was
no Baby Bear.

Olly threw a pile of leaves in the air.

He made pawprints in the flower beds.

He did some digging with Dad's spade.

It was fun.

Pitter patter,
pitter patter

“Oh!” said Olly. “It’s raining!”

The back door was shut. “Let me in!” shouted Olly.

But Mum and Dad couldn’t hear him.

Olly looked up at the kitchen window.
There was Baby Bear.

Baby Bear looked out and saw Olly.
She waved and waved!

"Goodness!"
said Mum.
"Olly's out in the rain!"

Dad let Olly in. Mum gave him a hot drink.
"Thank you, Baby Bear," said Olly.
"I'll play with you if you like."

"NO!" said Baby Bear.

And everyone laughed . . .

. . . but not for long!